From MARCELLA

12/81

WILLIAM COLLINS SONS & CO LTD
London Glasgow Sydney Auckland
Toronto Johannesburg

First published 1981
© Elizabeth Walter, 1981

Designed by Ronald Clark
Printed by W. S. Cowell Ltd, Ipswich

The illustrations of Victorian and
Edwardian Valentines and scraps are reproduced
by courtesy of Ronald Clark, The Mansell Collection,
The Mary Evans Picture Library,
The Victoria and Albert Museum
and Private Collections

ISBN 0 00 216863 4

Elizabeth Walter

requests the pleasure of your company for

A WEDDING BOUQUET

to celebrate your

Engagement/Marriage/Anniversary

and those of your friends

and relations

Collins

14 St James's Place

London sw1

ISBN 0 00 216863 4

PTO

WEDDING

There was nothing religious or sentimental about the original wedding. The word comes from the Anglo-Saxon *wed*, a pledge. This pledge was initially a financial one: the bride price, or sum of money paid by the bridegroom to the bride's father, which in turn had evolved from the compensation paid (sometimes) in an earlier age when prospective brides were simply carried off. The money was handed over when the couple exchanged vows, that is, plighted their troth, at betrothal – often while they were still children. The betrothal was as legally binding as a marriage.

Priests were often asked to witness betrothals and marriages (especially since some fathers had a tendency to sell the same daughter more than once), and a blessing was asked, but until the reign of Protestant Edward VI the

AUNT DEBORAH   PAPA   MAMA.   THE BEST MAN.   THE BRIDEGROOM.   LOVE

actual 'wedding' took place outside the church, in the churchyard or porch, before the company went in for the nuptial Mass. 'The Solemnization of Matrimony' is one of the seven sacraments of the Church but the Anglican service still incorporates the contractual wedding in such phrases as 'with this ring I thee wed . . . and thereto I plight thee my troth.'

There have been many versions of the vows exchanged at a wedding. One of the most charming is a mediaeval one in which the bride promised to be 'debonair and buxom, in bed and at board', debonair meaning good-humoured and buxom pliant and yielding – a description of the spirit which we now apply to the flesh.

Humble wedlock is far better than proud virginity. ST AUGUSTINE

A bachelor is a young unmarried man. In the Middle Ages, students were forbidden to marry, which explains why the first degree bestowed upon them was that of Bachelor of Arts. A young unmarried knight was a knight bachelor, and the company of such knights was known as the bachelery of England.

In the reign of Henry VIII Cardinal Reginald Pole suggested taxing bachelors in order to encourage them to become husbands and so increase the birthrate. The money thus raised was to provide family allowances for poor persons with large families, and dowries for indigent virgins.

Fortunately the insistence on celibacy no longer applies to the modern honour of Knight Bachelor conferred by the Queen.

Young unmarried daughters in the Middle Ages stayed at home and made themselves useful about the house. One of the most important household tasks was spinning wool to make the family's clothes. So the girls were known as spinners, or – to give the word its feminine ending – spinsters.

All reformers are bachelors.
GEORGE MOORE

'This year, next year, sometime, never.' Who has not repeated the childhood chant while counting plum stones round the edge of a plate, not to mention the chant of 'Tinker, tailor, soldier, sailor, rich man, poor man, beggarman, thief,' or one of its more sophisticated versions?

In the days when marriage was important to women for economic and social reasons, it is not surprising that they resorted to all kinds of methods of divination. Pulling the petals from a daisy to the accompaniment of 'He loves me, he loves me not' is one still practised, even if not seriously. Two teaspoons in a girl's saucer are also widely believed to foretell a wedding.

The really desperate could try a prayer to St Catherine of Alexandria, whose feast day is November 25. This virgin princess was bound to a wheel, which miraculously broke, thus ensuring her a more humane martyrdom by beheading. St Catherine is consequently the patron of all whose work is connected with wheels, and especially of unmarried girls who spent their time at the spinning-wheel. One prayer to her runs:

St Catherine, St Catherine, O
lend me thine aid,
And grant that I never may die
an old maid.
A husband, St Catherine.
Kind, St Catherine.
Tall, St Catherine.
Handsome, St Catherine.
Rich, St Catherine.
Soon, St Catherine.

PROPOSAL

Suitors on their knees beseeching the ladies of their choice to make them the happiest of men is a charming picture, but there is no knowing how many young men ever literally sank to their knees in the traditional posture of adoration and supplication, or even to one knee, the traditional posture of homage and fealty.

As for proposals themselves, they are so many and varied that whole books have been devoted to them. Yet their eloquence did not always call forth an unequivocal answer. The lady had the last word and would not necessarily give it.

Prithee, say aye or no;
If thou'lt not have me, tell me so;
I cannot stay
Nor will I wait upon
A smile or frown.
If thou wilt have me, say:
Then I am thine, or else I am my
own.

THOMAS SHIPMAN

ENGAGEMENT RING

A ring was an essential part of a betrothal. It was originally placed on the fourth finger of the girl's right hand and worn there until the wedding, when the bridegroom transferred it to the fourth finger of her left hand. So the same ring served for betrothal and wedding.

Sometimes a gimmal ring was used. This was a plain gold band consisting of two, sometimes three, separate rings, one for each partner and one for a witness, which could be fastened together by a pair of clasped hands to form a single ring – a reminder that another name for a betrothal was a handfasting.

The binding nature of betrothals was ended by the Marriage Act of 1754. The engagements which replaced them were much less serious affairs. As if to symbolize this difference, the plain gold band gave way to a more elaborate ring containing precious or semi-precious stones.

The most popular stones are: diamond, signifying lasting conjugal love; ruby, signifying contentment; emerald for hope; pearl for purity (or tears); amethyst for sincerity; sapphire for repentance; topaz for cheerfulness; garnet for constancy; turquoise for prosperity. Opals are thought to be unlucky except for those born in October, when they are said to signify lovableness.

It is considered very unlucky to lose or break an engagement ring.

Up, up, fair Bride, and call
Thy stars, from out their several boxes take
Thy Rubies, Pearls and Diamonds forth, and make
Thyself a constellation of them all.

JOHN DONNE

BANNS

'A man may not marry his grandmother' has become something of a joke, but in the Middle Ages the degrees of consanguinity forbidden by the Church were formidably complicated, and since there were no centralized records to refer to, it was only too easy for these degrees to be infringed, thus rendering the marriage invalid. To prevent this or any other last-minute hitches – still allowed for in the Anglican marriage service – an Archbishop of Canterbury in the early fourteenth century ordered the banns to be read in church. 'Bann' means proclamation. The banns were to be read for three consecutive Sundays before every wedding, and the marriage itself had to take place in church, in daylight, and in the face of the congregation. This was an attempt to prevent clandestine betrothals and marriages, and those known to be illegal but still performed by obliging priests.

It used to be thought very unlucky for an engaged couple to hear their banns called in church. Today their presence is expected on at least one occasion.

He who is about to marry is on the way to repentance. GREEK PROVERB

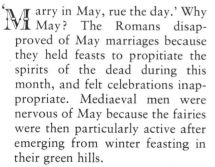

'Marry in May, rue the day.' Why May? The Romans disapproved of May marriages because they held feasts to propitiate the spirits of the dead during this month, and felt celebrations inappropriate. Mediaeval men were nervous of May because the fairies were then particularly active after emerging from winter feasting in their green hills.

Although the mediaeval Church had frowned on marriages during Lent, Advent and one or two other seasons, these restrictions rapidly disappeared after the Reformation. It is to the Victorians that we owe the restoration of Lent as a period of abstinence from marriage, and it was then that the tag 'Marry in Lent, live to repent' became current. Until very recently, the tax advantages to be gained by marrying shortly before the financial year ended on April 5 far outweighed religious considerations for most people. Legislation has now removed the tax advantages but the charm of a spring wedding still makes Lent a popular and acceptable season.

But if Lent is acceptable, Sunday is not. Because it was a holiday it was once the most popular day for weddings, but the Puritans put a stop to it in 1656 since there must be no merrymaking on a Sunday.

Though women are angels, yet wedlock's the devil. LORD BYRON

A ring has always been part of a wedding, even if it was only loaned for the ceremony itself. Indeed, the ring represented the original 'wed', or pledge placed on the fourth finger of the bride's left hand in the presence of priest and congregation. The Puritans, however, frowned on rings as relics of popery, and they were omitted from the marriage service in the *Directory of Publick Worship*, which replaced the *Book of Common Prayer* in 1656. Nevertheless, many people continued to use them, and the Restoration of the King in 1660 saw the official restoration of the ring also.

The fourth finger of the left hand was thought to be particularly suitable for the plain gold circle, symbol of unending love, because of a belief – alas, erroneous – that a vein, known as the *vena amoris*, ran from it straight to the heart.

To drop the ring during the wedding ceremony was an omen of dire disaster.

'With this ring I thee wed . . .'

How many torments lie in the small circle of a wedding ring. COLLEY CIBBER

'... AND SOMETHING NEW'

Something old and something new,
Something borrowed and something blue.

This best-known of all wedding rhymes, whose injunctions are faithfully observed by the majority of brides, is comparatively recent. It is not recorded before the second half of the nineteenth century.

'Something old and something new' symbolize the bride's old life and the new one on which she is now embarking. 'Something borrowed' symbolizes the community aspect of marriage, and also good neighbourhood. Blue is the colour of true religion and constancy, perhaps because it is traditionally the colour of the Virgin Mary's robe.

Some versions of the rhyme add 'And a silver sixpence in her shoe', the coin representing wealth and the shoe fertility.

Marriage is popular because it combines the maximum of temptation with
the maximum of opportunity.
GEORGE BERNARD SHAW

WEDDING DRESS

Every bride who could possibly afford it had a new dress in which to begin her new life, the finer the better, but it wasn't necessarily impractical white. Far from wearing it once only, she expected (unless she was very rich) that it would do duty as her best dress for several years to come. The white wedding, which we think of as universal and traditional, is largely a nineteenth-century creation.

Whatever the colour, numerous superstitions attach to the wedding dress. It is unlucky to try it on in its entirety before it is donned for the wedding. For this reason a few stitches are often left to be added at the last minute. Nor should dress and veil be tried on together, for this is tempting fate. Above all, the bride must not survey herself in the mirror in full panoply until just before she leaves for church.

We women, dressed . . . in virgin white on our wedding-days, seem
but like milk-white heifers led to sacrifice.
SAMUEL RICHARDSON

COLOURS

Few brides would risk marrying in green: it is thought to be unlucky and she who wears green will soon wear mourning. Green is the fairy colour, and the little people in the green hills were much feared in earlier centuries. To wear their colour might give them some hold over the wearer.

White denotes purity and is the sacred colour. This explains why nightwear was almost always white: the holy colour warded off evil spirits who might prey upon the unconscious – and therefore vulnerable – sleeper.

Silver was originally for royal brides. The Princess Elizabeth, daughter of James I, wore a sumptuous silver dress at her wedding to the Elector Palatine on St Valentine's Day, 1613. No daughter of a reigning monarch married again until the eldest daughter of George II in 1734. Since the Hanoverian claim to the throne derived from this same Princess Elizabeth, white and silver were chosen for the bride's dress in compliment to her ancestress. The eldest daughters of George III and George IV were also married in silver, or white and silver. Though Queen Victoria broke with this tradition by marrying in white, the popularity of silver spread down the social scale. It is now the accepted colour for bridal accessories.

Blue, denoting constancy, has always been a favourite choice. Yellow, the Roman marriage colour, is also favourable, and so are red, pink and lilac.

It is very unlucky for anyone to wear black, however elegant, at a wedding because it is the colour of mourning. The same applies to purple.

Though marriage makes man and wife one flesh, it leaves 'em still two fools.
WILLIAM CONGREVE

BRIDAL VEIL

I consider everybody as having a right to marry once in their lives for love, if they can.
JANE AUSTEN

Roman brides went veiled to their weddings, and the veil was yellow, the colour sacred to Hymen, god of marriage. But the custom died out with the Romans and brides in England went unveiled until the revival of classical styles of dress in the early nineteenth century, though the veil worn then was more of a trailing scarf of light material than the tulle or lace confection we know today. The idea of veiling the blushing virginal face only came in during the 1860s as part of the Victorian cult of the white wedding, and the custom of arriving veiled at the church on a father's arm and leaving it unveiled and triumphant on a husband's is more recent still.

The veil often represents the 'something borrowed' of the modern bride. An old veil is thought to be luckier than a new one, especially if it has been worn by a happily married close relative. A veil of beautiful Honiton or Brussels lace is often a family heirloom, handed down from mother to daughter.

Royal brides do not arrive veiled at church. The public expect to see their faces. Some say that this tradition derives from a time when precautions had to be taken against any last-minute substitution.

WEDDING BOUQUET

From earliest times flowers have been an integral part of weddings. Bride and groom were both garlanded at Roman and Anglo-Saxon weddings. In the Middle Ages children often strewed flowers before the bride as she emerged from church – a custom commemorated in the name flower-girl for a junior bridal attendant. The church is decorated with flowers; the bridesmaids carry them; and of course there is the bride's bouquet, whether posy, spray or sheaf.

The Victorians invested every flower with its own meaning. Some modern brides might be surprised to know what their bouquets spell out. The ever-popular rose symbolizes love, and a white rose, 'I am worthy of you.' The white lily stands for purity and sweetness, the lily of the valley for the return of happiness, the myrtle, like the rose, symbolizes love, and orange blossom proclaims, 'Your purity equals your loveliness.' Both myrtle (sacred to Venus) and orange blossom (orange trees bear prolifically) were originally fertility symbols. Carnations can be an unfortunate choice, for though pink ones symbolize woman's love, red ones mean, 'Alas for my poor heart,' and yellow ones disdain. Chrysanthemums too have snags: red ones mean, 'I love,' and white ones truth, but who would want to carry yellow chrysanthemums announcing slighted love?

Flowers were such a symbol of the bride that if an engaged girl died before her wedding a garland of real or imitation flowers was carried at her funeral and afterwards hung in the church.

O, the red rose whispers of passion,
And the white rose breathes of love.
O, the red rose is a falcon,
And the white rose is a dove.

But I send you a cream-white rosebud
With a flush on its petal tips,
For the love that is purest and sweetest
Has a kiss of desire on the lips.

JOHN BOYLE O'REILLY

A bridegroom originally 'won' his bride by carrying her off by force. He was one of a raiding party and there was no wooing or ceremony about it. As times grew more civilized and the abduction became transformed into a wedding, with legal safeguards, the bridegroom's raiding companions became transformed into a group of young bachelors who attended him at his wedding and were known as groomsmen – though their role remained defensive, since a rival suitor might come raiding in his turn and carry off the bride, and if a wedding took place without the consent of the bride's family, her male relatives might descend in a body and snatch her back.

By the nineteenth century, when the groomsmen had dwindled to mere ceremonial attendants, one in particular began to be singled out as Best Man and took charge of those practical arrangements, such as safeguarding the ring and paying the parson, which the bridegroom – for whatever reason – was deemed in no fit state to carry out.

A young man married is a man that's marred. WILLIAM SHAKESPEARE

BRIDESMAIDS

Roman brides were attended by Roman matrons, but at Anglo-Saxon weddings the attendants were unmarried girls, contemporaries of the bride. These 'bride maidens' helped in making the garlands with which bride and groom were crowned. They also formed a defensive bodyguard for the bride, making it more difficult for her to be carried off. Although one of them is now designated chief bridesmaid and holds the bride's bouquet during the exchange of vows and the signing of the register, the bridesmaids have not suffered the same reduction as the groomsmen and still usually number two or three.

After the ceremony the bride sometimes throws her bouquet (originally her slipper) among them, and the one to secure it will be the next to marry – provided she hasn't been a bridesmaid more than three times. 'Always a bridesmaid, never a bride' is a well-known caveat.

A happy bridesmaid makes a happy bride. ALFRED, LORD TENNYSON

WEDDING FAVOURS

The white carnations supplied to wedding guests for buttonhole or corsage are the last vestige of one of the oldest wedding customs: the wearing of wedding favours. Favours in a lady's colours had long been an accepted way for a man to declare publicly his interest. Knights jousting in a tournament often wore a knot of ribbons in their chosen lady's colours, and originally the favours worn at weddings were also gaily coloured, often in the same colours as the bride's dress.

Favours were usually handed out by the bridesmaids as the guests left the church, or while the register was being signed, but the principals wore them for the ceremony itself. In the eighteenth century, when the vogue for white weddings first came in, the favours too turned pale, and bridegroom and grooms-men wore flat white satin bows on the shoulder. If they were in uniform, the bows were attached to the epaulettes. They were worn on naval uniform by the Duke of York (later George V) at his wedding to Princess May of Teck in 1893, but by the time their daughter Mary married the Earl of Harewood in 1922 all too many men had married in uniform during the 1914–18 war, favours had disappeared, and the custom has never been revived.

What woman, however old, has not the bridal-favours and raiment stowed away, and packed in lavender, in the inmost cupboards of her heart.
WILLIAM MAKEPEACE THACKERAY

WEDDING MUSIC

Music may be the food of love, but it was a late-comer on the wedding scene. Church weddings began as quiet early-morning affairs, with friends invited to breakfast afterwards. It was the Victorians who expanded them into the form familiar today, with a packed church and large reception to follow. Music, whether organ or choral, both entertained the congregation and alerted them to dramatic moments in the ceremony.

Certain pieces rapidly established themselves as essential bridal music. Chief among them is the wedding march (or rather, the Bridal Chorus) from Wagner's opera *Lohengrin*. Since it was first performed at Weimar in 1850, innumerable brides have entered or left church to the strains of 'Here comes the Bride.' In 1889 it was played at a royal marriage: that of the Prince of Wales's daughter,

Princess Louise, when it replaced the previous herald of the bride, Handel's *Occasional Overture*.

An even earlier favourite was the wedding march from Mendelssohn's incidental music to *A Midsummer Night's Dream*. Composed in 1826, the music was published by Novello's in 1847 as a piano duet and was almost immediately adapted for the organ. It was played at the wedding of Queen Victoria's eldest daughter in 1858 and has never lost its popularity.

Other favourite Victorian wedding music included Handel's *Processional March* and the march from *Hercules*, Mendelssohn's march from *Athalie,* and Beethoven's Hallelujah Chorus from *The Mount of Olives*. More recently, Bach's *Jesu, Joy of Man's Desiring* and the Triumphal March from Verdi's *Aida* have proved popular.

Marriage the happiest bond of love might be
If hands were only joined when hearts agree.
LORD LANSDOWNE

WEDDING BELLS

A joyful peal of bells as the bride leaves the church on her husband's arm is one of the oldest wedding traditions. The bells made 'a joyful noise unto the Lord'; before the age of widespread literacy and newspapers they signified to the whole parish that the wedding had taken place; and they added to the general air of festivity.

None of these rationalizations is the real reason why a peal is rung.

A wedding is a beginning, and the beginning of any new enterprise was always considered hazardous because evil spirits might slip in and cause the whole undertaking to miscarry. So long before the Christian era people gathered at weddings with every noise-making object they could lay hands on to create an unholy din which would drive the evil spirits away.

In due course the Church, ever quick to adapt old ways to its own advantage, substituted the noise made by sanctified bells and tactfully omitted mention of evil spirits.

Like blude, like gude, like age makes the happy marriage. SCOTTISH PROVERB

HUSBANDS AND ...

The notion of a good provider is inherent in the word husband. The word originally meant master or manager of the house, hence one who is thrifty and careful. We still speak of husbanding one's resources, or husbandry meaning farm management.

What about a wife? She began by being just an older woman, not necessarily married, as in goodwife, fishwife, midwife, or even housewife. But a man's woman, when thus singled out, soon became something more, and in no time the Church was declaring 'I now pronounce you man and wife.'

> *In true marriage lies*
> *Nor equal or unequal; each fulfils*
> *Defect in each, and always thought in thought,*
> *Purpose in purpose, will in will, they grow,*
> *The single pure and perfect animal,*
> *The two-cell'd heart beating, with one full stroke,*
> *Life.*

ALFRED, LORD TENNYSON

WIVES

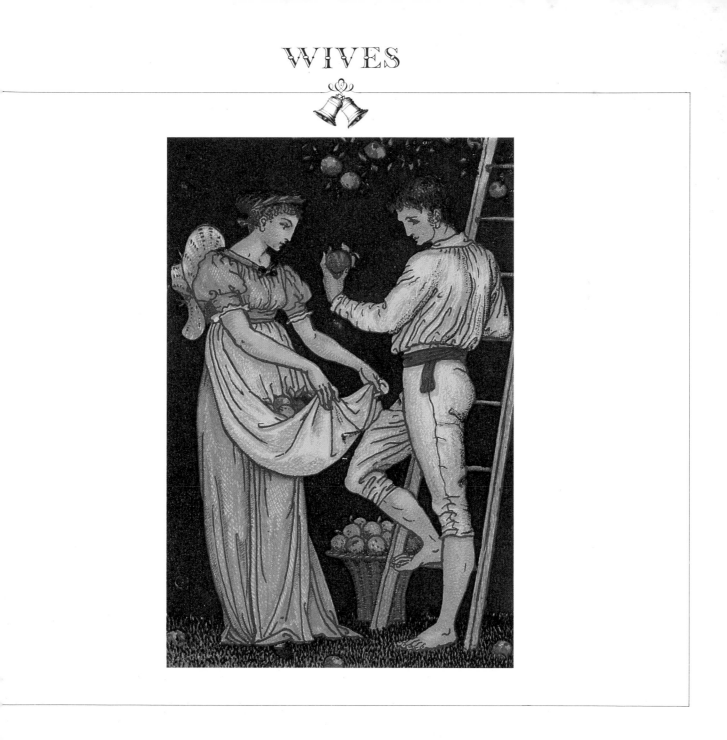

CONFETTI

Brides have always had things thrown at them – slippers, cakes, rice, to name but three. Today's bride is luckier: she is only pelted with confetti.

Confetti is Italian for confectionery – the tiny cakes and bonbons thrown among the crowd at carnivals and often made in the shape of hearts, flowers and good luck symbols. Sometimes the *confetti* themselves became symbolic and were made of paper.

The custom in England of showering bride and groom with paper slippers, horseshoes, rose petals, etcetera, began early this century, but tiny circles of tissue paper soon proved even cheaper.

Computer punchings are cheaper still, if harder, as some couples can testify.

The shower of paper blessings in whatever shape is one more custom intended to bestow fertility on the newly married couple.

Of all actions of a man's life, his marriage does least concern other people;
yet of all actions of our life, 'tis most meddled with by other people.
SIR JOHN SELDEN

THE BEST OF LUCK

Good luck is never more desirable than in married life, and representations of horseshoes and black cats, the traditional luck-bringers, are presented to many brides. Another sign of great good fortune is for a wedding party to meet a chimney-sweep carrying his brushes and with soot-blackened face, though in these days of central heating such encounters are increasingly rare. Prince Philip made the most of one when a sweep passed by Buckingham Palace shortly before his marriage to the Queen (then Princess Elizabeth): he went down and shook hands with him.

It is very important that the wedding party should *meet* the sweep; to see his back view is exceedingly unlucky. The sweep must be greeted in some way, and ideally he should turn and walk a little way with the procession.

The sweep is considered a bringer of good fortune because he is connected with fire and the hearth, essential symbols of warmth, light and home. A bride on entering her new home used to be ceremonially handed the fire-irons as a sign that she was now the mistress of hearth and home.

The sun is another happy omen connected with fire and light, and a sunny wedding day is fortunate as well as pleasant.

Blest is the bride on whom the sun doth shine. ROBERT HERRICK

WEDDING BREAKFAST

Marriage was a sacrament and one therefore received it fasting. Except by special licence, weddings could be performed in church only between 8.00 a.m. and twelve noon until 1885, when the hours were extended to 3.00 p.m. Even so, there was often a demand for an early ceremony to give the happy pair a chance to make their journey, so the celebratory feast came to be known as the wedding breakfast, even though it more usually resembled a luncheon.

Charles Lamb, attending an 8.00 a.m. wedding in 1821, described the 'protracted breakfast of three hours' as consisting of 'cold fowls, tongues, hams, botargoes [roes of red mullet], dried fruits, wines, cordials, etc.'

The extension of the hours to 6.00 p.m. in 1934 spelled the end of the wedding breakfast. Today the festive gathering is known universally as a reception, and improved transport facilities mean that the honeymooners can leave late in the day and still reach their destination.

Mrs Beeton gives the menu opposite for a Victorian wedding breakfast.

The man must combine the distinguishing characteristics of an alderman and a boa-constrictor, who can dine happily after the violent delights and cloying pleasures of a wedding-luncheon.
JOHN CORDY JEAFFRESON

Oyster Patties
Fillets of Sole in Jelly
or
Russian Timbale of Turbot
Lobster Salad
Chicken Creams
Foie Gras Creams
Lamb Cutlets
Roast Chickens
or
Stuffed Turkey Poult
Pigeon Pie
Galantine of Veal
Ham and Tongue
Spiced Beef
Salad
Apricot Cream
or
Pistachio Cream
Mixed Fruit with Kirsch
Bananas in Jelly
Pineapple Charlotte
Meringues with Cream
French Pastry
Neapolitan Ice
Strawberry Cream
Fruit
Dessert
Coffee

WEDDING CAKE

Cake has been part of the marriage feast from earliest times. The Greeks and Romans both consumed ceremonial cakes made from wheat. Later the cake became a kind of spiced bread or biscuit of wheaten flour. By Tudor times sugar, eggs and currants were added. In the early seventeenth century Thomas Campion listed it among the attributes of a good housewife that she could 'trim with plums a bridal cake'.

Originally 'bride cakes' were small, and were thrown at the bride as she entered her new home. After the Restoration the fashion came from France of covering a pile of bride cakes with marzipan and sugar to form one large cake, and a London pastrycook on Ludgate Hill, who made cakes for the many illegal marriages conducted near the Fleet prison, had the bright idea of copying Wren's new spire for St Bride's Church. This is the alleged origin of the tiered wedding cake.

The cake is yet another fertility symbol. If a bride does not cut her own cake the marriage will be childless. To refuse an offered piece of cake is very unlucky. To sleep with a piece under the pillow will promote a girl's dreams of her future husband.

The custom of sending cake to those unable to attend the ceremony is not just courtesy: it ensures them a share of the luck which was scattered among the guests when the bride cakes thrown at the bride rained down on them and were scrambled for.

Marriage has many pains, but celibacy has no pleasures. SAMUEL JOHNSON

Old boots and shoes attached to the going-away car have followed many couples for the first few yards of married life. The Victorians threw them after the departing pair for luck, particularly the bride's own wedding slippers, and it was considered especially lucky to hit the carriage, or even the bride or groom. Queen Victoria described how the Prince of Wales (later Edward VII) and Princess Alexandra drove off from Windsor in a shower of slippers.

Shoes have always played a part in wedding ceremonies. Roman brides wore yellow shoes as well as a yellow veil in honour of Hymen. At Anglo-Saxon weddings the bride's father handed one of her shoes to the bridegroom, who tapped her on the head with it to signal that he was now her master. (Was he reminding her that the victor customarily placed his foot on the vanquished's neck?)

The bride herself also did her share of shoe-throwing. She flung her right shoe among the bridesmaids and whoever caught it would be next to marry. Today she throws her bouquet instead.

No one knows why shoes were so prominent in wedding ceremonies. One theory is that a slipper resembles the womb in shape and was thus one more fertility symbol.

Most men and most women are merely one couple more. RALPH WALDO EMERSON

HONEYMOON

Honeymoon (originally honey-month) described the first few weeks of married bliss, after which it was said to wane.

The earliest recorded English honeymoon is that of William Marshal, who in 1189 married the heiress of the Earl of Pembroke, through whom he inherited the title. Immediately after the wedding he took his bride to the manor of Stoke d'Abernon in Surrey, the home of Sir Engerrand d'Abernon, described by a contemporary as a 'peaceful, comfortable and delightful spot'.

But only those who made such advantageous marriages as William Marshal could afford to honeymoon. Most couples moved into their new home straight away and were back at work next morning. Gradually, as economic circumstances improved, it became usual to spend a few days in seclusion, either at home or in a house lent by a friend. By the beginning of the nineteenth century it had become customary for those who could afford it to take a trip – to the seaside, to a fashionable watering place, or to London. As the century wore on and methods of transport improved, the trip became a tour, or even a Grand Tour lasting several months.

The original somewhat derisory connotation of honeymoon meant that the word did not become socially acceptable until well into the nineteenth century. Going away, wedding tour or bridal tour were all preferred. We have preserved the first expression in describing the bride's travelling outfit as her going-away dress.

When people are tied up for life, 'tis in their mutual interest not to grow weary of one another.
LADY MARY WORTLEY MONTAGUE

SPECIAL CASES

Special licences, allowing a couple to be married by a clergyman in any church, at any time of day, and without the calling of banns beforehand, have been in existence since the fourteenth century. They became particularly popular in the eighteenth century, when there was a vogue for quiet, secret weddings, often held in the bride's home. Special licences are issued only by the Archbishop of Canterbury, and only in circumstances approved by him – for example, embarkation leave during the war.

In Scotland no licence or special licence is required, and weddings can be held at any time and in any place, provided certain residential qualifications are observed.

Because Scotland was outside the Marriage Act of 1754 which put an end to the many hasty and irregular marriages conducted by unfrocked priests, it rapidly became the goal of all couples desirous of contracting such unions, and where better than Gretna Green, just over the border from Carlisle. There is some doubt whether the celebrant at Gretna was actually a blacksmith, but none that many marriages were celebrated in his forge.

It is better to marry than to burn. ST PAUL

SECULAR MARRIAGE

Once the Church had transformed weddings into holy matrimony it insisted that the only lawful marriages were those solemnized in church, and – after the Reformation – the Anglican church at that. Catholics and Dissenters might have their own ceremony if they wished, but they had to have an Anglican one as well. As for secular weddings, they did not exist.

The Puritans changed all that. When they came to power during the Protectorate they banned church weddings, and from 1653 to 1656 marriages could only be performed before a justice of the peace, though the banns might still be called in church if the couple preferred that to the alternative of the market-place. After 1656 church weddings were again accepted, though not the marriage service in the *Book of Common Prayer*. That had to wait until 1660, when the King enjoyed his own again.

The Marriage Act of 1754 exempted Jews and Quakers from the need to have an official Anglican ceremony, but other Dissenters and Roman Catholics had to wait until 1836 before marriages in their places of worship were legally recognized.

In the same year the machinery for civil marriage was introduced. Registrars and register offices were created, and for the first time secular marriage was available for those who did not want a religious ceremony.

Marriage is a step so grave and decisive that it attracts light-headed,
variable men by its very awfulness.
ROBERT LOUIS STEVENSON

In the United States weddings have always been held at home if the couple prefer it – and many still do. This custom is in part a survival from the past: the early Puritan settlers took with them their dislike of ostentatious weddings, and civil marriage was common in New England in the seventeenth century. Since it was the person of the magistrate that was important rather than a specific building, weddings tended

to be celebrated in the bride's home as a matter of convenience. Even brides who would have liked a church ceremony had often to forgo it, for the nearest church might be many miles away. Ministers recognized the difficulty, and before long they too were ready to conduct weddings in a place of the couple's choice.

Wives are young men's mistresses, companions for middle age, and old men's nurses.
FRANCIS BACON

The custom of carrying the bride across the threshold of her new home dates back to Roman times, when it was said to have commemorated the rape of the Sabine women, from which forced union the Romans themselves were descended.

Another explanation is that it was done to avoid ill luck, since it was considered exceedingly unlucky to stumble when entering a house.

Originally the bride was lifted over the threshold by members of the wedding party. Today's bridegroom is expected to do it single-handed. Perhaps brides are slimmer now?

That's what a man wants in a wife, mostly: he wants to
make sure o' one fool as'll tell him he's wise.
GEORGE ELIOT

ENVOI

Blessings in abundance come
To the Bride and to her Groom;
May the bed and this short night
Know the fullness of delight!
Pleasures many here attend ye,
And ere long a Boy Love send ye,
Curled and comely and so trim
Maids (in time) may ravish him.
Thus a dew of Graces fall
On ye both; Goodnight to all.
ROBERT HERRICK

and they lived . . .

…HAPPILY EVER AFTER

M arried couples have the following anniversaries to look forward to:

1st	Paper	13th	Lace
2nd	Cotton	14th	Ivory
3rd	Leather	15th	Crystal
4th	Silk (or Flowers)	20th	China
5th	Wood	25th	Silver
6th	Iron	30th	Pearl
7th	Copper	35th	Coral
8th	Bronze (or Rubber)	40th	Ruby
9th	Pottery	45th	Sapphire
10th	Tin (or Aluminium)	50th	Gold
11th	Steel	55th	Emerald
12th	Linen	60th	Diamond

Early marriage, long love. GERMAN PROVERB

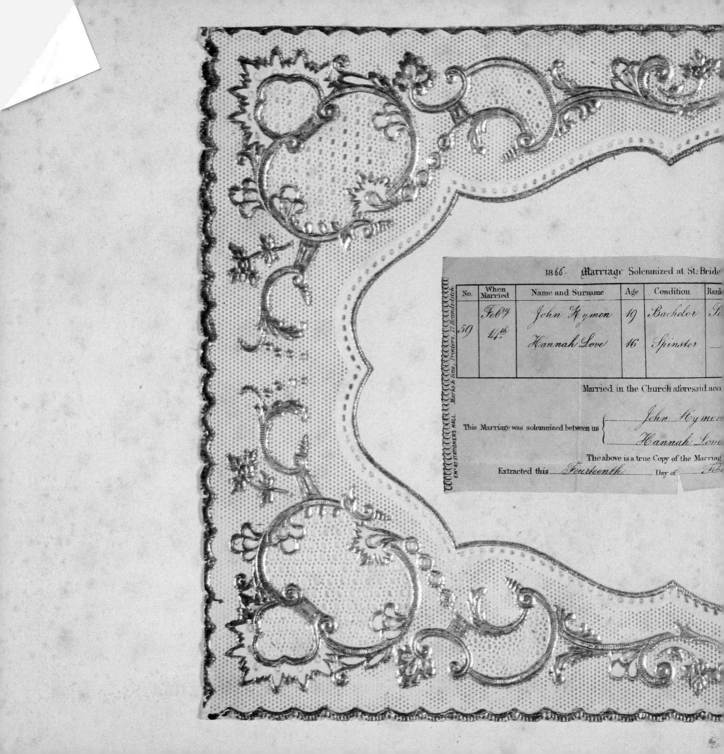

1866. **Marriage** Solemnized at St: Bride'

No.	When Married	Name and Surname	Age	Condition	Rank
59	Feb.y 14.th	John Hymen	19	Bachelor	
		Hannah Love	16	Spinster	—

Married in the Church aforesaid acc

This Marriage was solemnized between us { John Hymen

Hannah Love

The above is a true Copy of the Marring

Extracted this *Fourteenth* Day of Feb

ENG.D AT STATIONER'S HALL. Marsh & Sons, Printers, 72 Friendistlich